The Ker

D0894562

ɔn S

THIS BOOK BELONGS TO

_____
name

EXTINCT FOR 65 MILLION YEARS, THEY'RE BACK!

Jurassic Park is a totally unique "zoo" located on Nublar Island, about 125 miles (200 km) off the coast of Costa Rica, in Central America. The fulfillment of five years work, is a dream come true for John Hammond, a businessman who made his fortune creating theme parks and zoos around the world.

Imagine an island covered with lush vegetation and inhabited by . . .
LIVE DINOSAURS!

HOW JURASSIC PARK BEGAN

First, paleontologists discovered dinosaur-age fossil mosquitoes (blood-sucking insects) preserved in chunks of amber. The insects' stomachs still contained the preserved blood of dinosaurs they bit more than 65 million years ago. Genetic scientists were then able to remove the ancient dinosaur DNA (the genetic code that acts as a blueprint for creating life) and, with the help of powerful computers, they created living dinosaur embryos.

Dinosaurs are a group of ancient reptiles that lived on the Earth long before human beings appeared. No one had ever seen a living dinosaur before . . . until now!

United States

— **Mexico**

Costa Rica —

South America

Brachiosaur pen 2

Main road

Velociraptors pit

Visitor center

T. rex paddock

Dilophosaurus pen

Dock

Access road

Vista view

Helipad

Brachiosaur pen 1

Visitors tour Jurassic Park in specially equipped cars called Explorers. Absolutely everything on the island is run by the computer control center – even the cars! The island has an ultra high-tech security system that utilizes movement sensors, electric fences, enormous cement ditches and protected pens to keep the dinosaurs away from humans.

The only oasis of civilization in the thick forest of the island is the visitors compound, where Jurassic Park guests stay. It also houses the control room and laboratory, as well as the Jurassic Park Center. The whole area is surrounded by a set of giant electric fences to protect people from unwanted visitors. The Raptor pen, where the small and dangerous Velociraptors live, is located near the compound.

THE STORY BEGINS

The group of scientists and visitors arriving at Jurassic Park are about to be the first to tour the park and see living dinosaurs, before the official opening.

The weather is beautiful now, but a tropical storm is heading for the island at lightning speed.

Everything seems fine, but things are about to go very wrong . . .

HERE ARE THE EIGHT CHARACTERS WHO WILL EXPLORE JURASSIC PARK WITH YOU

DR. ELLIE SATTLER

Dr. Ellie Sattler is a paleobotanist, a scientist who studies fossil plants. She's come to Jurassic Park to assist Dr. Grant with the inspection.

TIM

Tim is the nine-year-old grandson of John Hammond. A big dinosaur buff, he's on the island to visit his grandpa — and Dr. Grant, his hero.

DR. ALAN GRANT

Dr. Alan Grant, a paleontologist who studies the skeletons and behavior of carnivorous dinosaurs, has been invited to Jurassic Park to inspect the facilities before the official park opening.

JOHN HAMMOND

John Hammond is a billionaire business-man who accom-plished his dream to build Jurassic Park. Totally obsessed by dinosaurs, he has invented a new kind of theme park. His company, InGen Corporation, created Jurassic Park and all its dinosaurs.

DR. IAN MALCOLM

Dr. Ian Malcolm is a mathematical genius here to inspect the operations. However, he doesn't believe that science can always control complex natural systems. He's certain that something will eventually go wrong with the park.

DENNIS NEDRY

Dennis Nedry programmed all the computer systems in Jurassic Park. He secretly decided to sell frozen dinosaur embryos to a rival company for a lot of money. To sneak the embryos off the island, he uses the computer to turn off the Jurassic Park security system. Unfortunately, his program eventually shuts down all island control systems. Now none of the electric fences are operational and the dinosaurs will soon discover that they can escape!

ALEXIS (LEX)

Lex is Tim's 12-year-old sister. She's as crazy about computers as Tim is about dinosaurs, and she has a crush on Dr. Grant.

ROBERT MULDOON

Robert Muldoon is the island game warden. Although he's worked with dangerous wild animals for years, he doesn't trust the dinosaurs — especially the Velociraptors.

NOW, IT'S TIME TO MEET ONE OF THE INHABITANTS OF JURASSIC PARK . . .

Early in their tour of Jurassic Park, the visitors get a chance to see the laboratory where all the dinosaurs are "made". The scientists and John Hammond enter the hatchery where baby dinosaurs are born. A cluster of hatching eggs is in an incubator.

After studying fossil Velociraptors for years, Dr. Grant gets a unique and unexpected opportunity: watching baby Velociraptors hatch — very much alive!

VELOCIRAPTOR

Meaning of name:
Fast or Swift Thief
Lived 75 million years ago
Carnivorous, Saurischian Dinosaur
Family Dromaeosauridae
Found in Asia (with close relatives in North America)
First discovered in 1922, in Mongolia
Scientifically described by Dr. H.F. Osborn in 1924
Maximum known body size:
6 feet / 2 meters long, 4 feet / 1.8 meters tall
Skull length: 8 inches / 0.2 meter long
Weight: 200 pounds / 90 kilograms

UTAHRAPTOR ostrommaysi
Meaning of name:
Ostrom and Mays' Utah Thief
Lived 125 million years ago
Carnivorous, Saurischian Dinosaur
Family Dromaeosauridae
Found in North America (with close relatives in Asia)
First discovered in 1992, in Utah
Scientifically described by Dr. Jim Kirkland in 1992
Maximum known body size:
20 feet / 6 meters long, 9 feet / 2.7 meters tall
Skull length: 1 foot 6 in. / 0.5 meter
Weight: 500 pounds / 227 kilograms

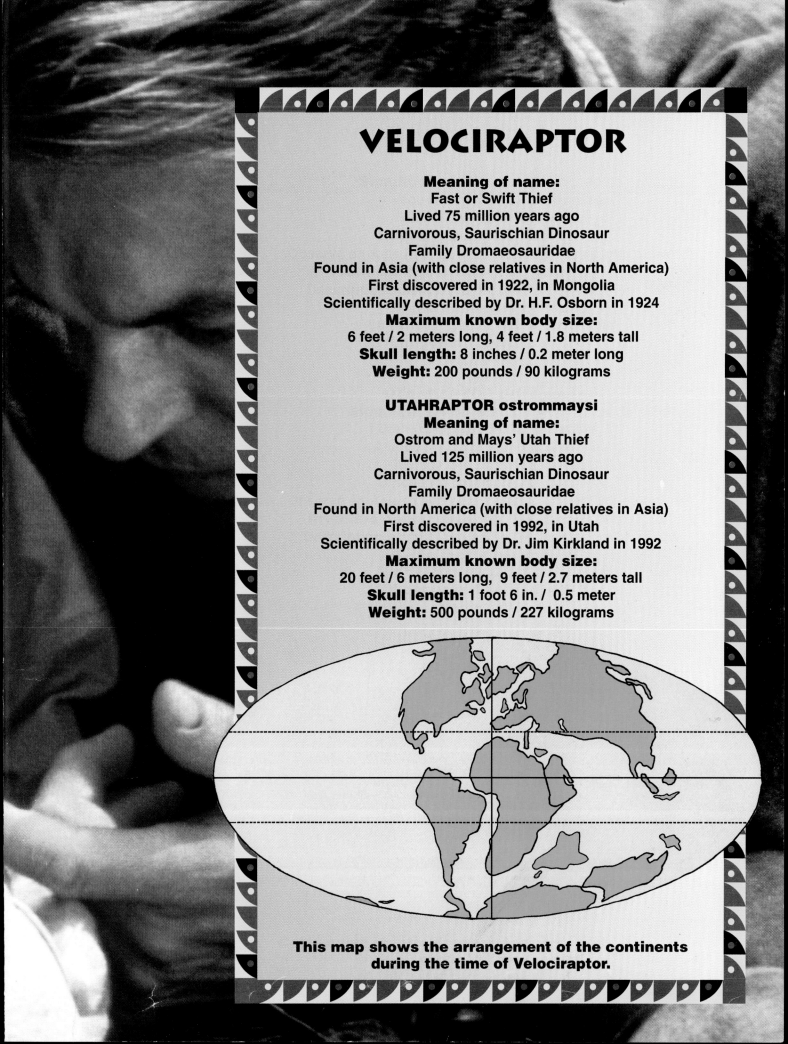

This map shows the arrangement of the continents during the time of Velociraptor.

Since the beginning of Jurassic Park, Mr. Hammond has closely watched the progress of the genetic scientists who create his dinosaurs. He watches the hatching of each egg with great emotion, and has seen the birth of every dinosaur in Jurassic Park.

Velociraptor and its close cousin Utahraptor belong to a group of dinosaurs known as the Dromaeosaurs. The Dromaeosaurs were a group of medium to small-sized meat-eating dinosaurs with several specialized features. They are very closely related to modern birds. In fact, some scientists have placed birds and Dromaeosaurs together in one large group.

The giant of the Dromaeosaurs was the recently discovered Utahraptor. It was found in 1992 in Utah. Although only about 10 per cent of the skeleton has been found, it is enough to give scientists a very good picture of Utahraptor.

The size of a full-sized adult Velociraptor compared to a six-foot (1.85 m) human.

The Velociraptor, nicknamed Raptor, is an extremely dangerous animal, so dangerous that it cannot live with any other species.

In Jurassic Park, the Velociraptors are penned in a special, highly protected area. These animals are very intelligent and constantly check their fence for weaknesses.

When Mr. Nedry causes the park security system to shut down, it's not long before the Velociraptors realize they have an opportunity to escape.

This map shows where the bones of Velociraptor and its North American cousins, Deinonychus, Saurornitholestes and Utahraptor, have been found.

Velociraptor is found in rock deposits all over central Asia. Dromaeosaurs, the family of meat-eating dinosaurs to which Velociraptor belongs, ranged over most of Asia and North America. The North American Dromaeosaurs have all been found in rocks along the western edge of the continent. Their wide variety and the great length of time this family is known to have existed indicates that Dromaeosaurs were a very successful group of animals.

The world that Velociraptor inhabited was semi-arid forest and sandy desert. This type of environment, with blowing dust and sand, was very good at burying, and therefore preserving, dinosaur skeletons.

To get the park systems up and running again, someone must go to the power room and turn the main switches back on. Decisively, Dr. Sattler rushes outside the main building to find the door to the basement power room. To her horror, she sees a giant hole in the Velociraptor fence — they've escaped!

She dashes to the power room and manages to get the power back on, but the biggest of the Velociraptors lurks in the shadows. On seeing it, she runs to escape and finally manages to return safely to the control room.

Meanwhile, Lex, Tim and Dr. Grant, who were caught in the park after the Tyrannosaurus attack, manage to return to the Park Center. They climb one of the non-functioning electric fences, without knowing Dr. Sattler is trying to turn the power back on. Reaching the other side just in time, they think they are safe — but two more Velociraptors are loose. Dr. Grant leaves Tim and Lex in the restaurant and goes for help.

Soon after Dr. Grant leaves, two Velociraptors enter the main building and pursue the children, who run into the kitchen shutting the door behind them. With their extraordinary sense of smell, the Velociraptors track them down . . .

Velociraptor had several skeletal adaptations that made it an effective hunter. The first, and most obvious, is the tremendous set of claws on its hands and feet. Although these claws were all long and sharp, there was a particularly nasty-looking one on each foot. The big inner toe had a claw on it that was like a giant razor-sharp sickle, held off the ground while walking or running so the claw was not dulled. The real purpose of this toe was for slashing and cutting. For this reason, some scientists have referred to Velociraptor as the "Freddy Kruger" of the dinosaur age.

When the fast moving Velociraptor ran after its next meal, it would change speed and direction many times to catch a dinosaur performing evasive maneuvers. This meant that the Velociraptor needed something to help it keep its balance, even during drastic movements. Like many animals that walk on their hind legs, Velociraptor used its tail as a counterbalance. To limit their flexibility, the tail bones were modified to mesh together. The modifications took the form of long thin rods of bone growing from one tail bone to the next. These structures allowed the tail to form a rod-like structure the Velociraptor could flick around as a counterbalance when changing direction while running.

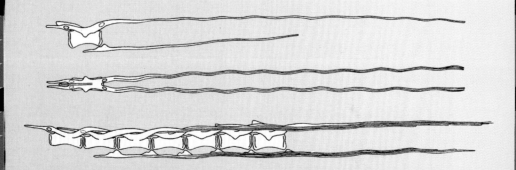

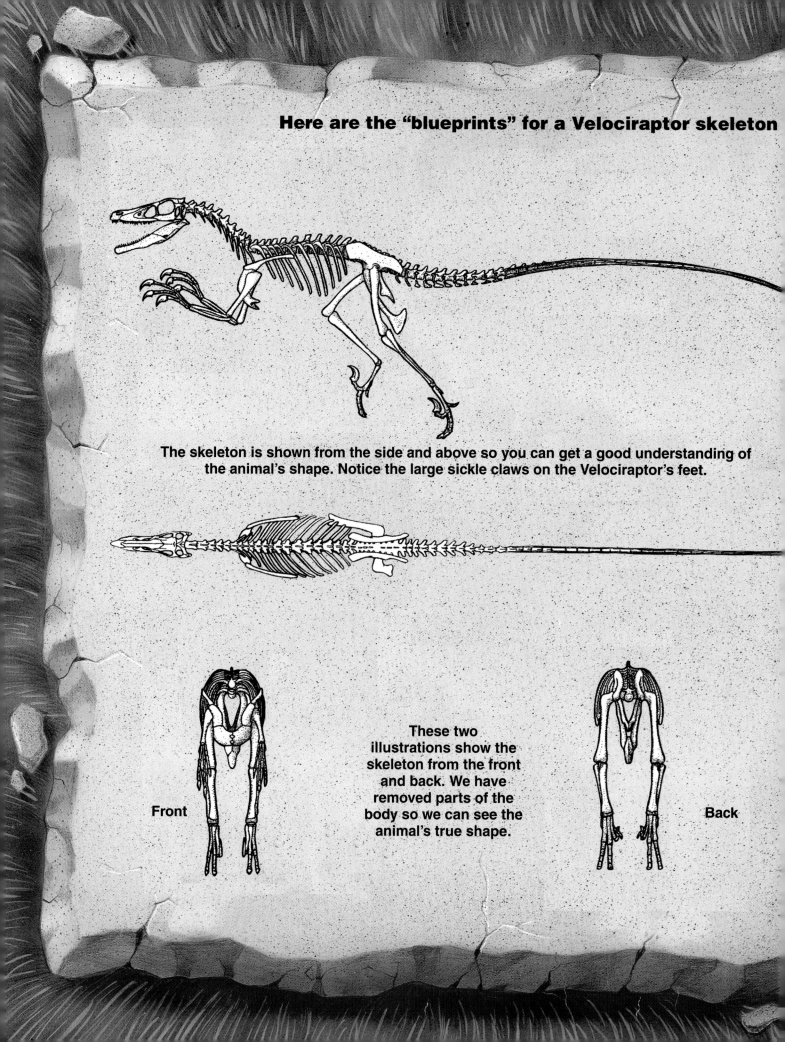

Here are the "blueprints" for a Velociraptor skeleton

The skeleton is shown from the side and above so you can get a good understanding of the animal's shape. Notice the large sickle claws on the Velociraptor's feet.

Front

These two illustrations show the skeleton from the front and back. We have removed parts of the body so we can see the animal's true shape.

Back

and the muscles that cover its bones.

The powerful muscles of Velociraptor allowed it to both hold up its weight and be a fast-moving hunter. Every animal with a backbone uses its hard skeleton to anchor the muscles. Scientists reconstruct the appearance of dinosaurs by examining fossil bones for the marks left by the muscle attachments and by comparing them to the modern cousins of the dinosaur — crocodiles and birds.

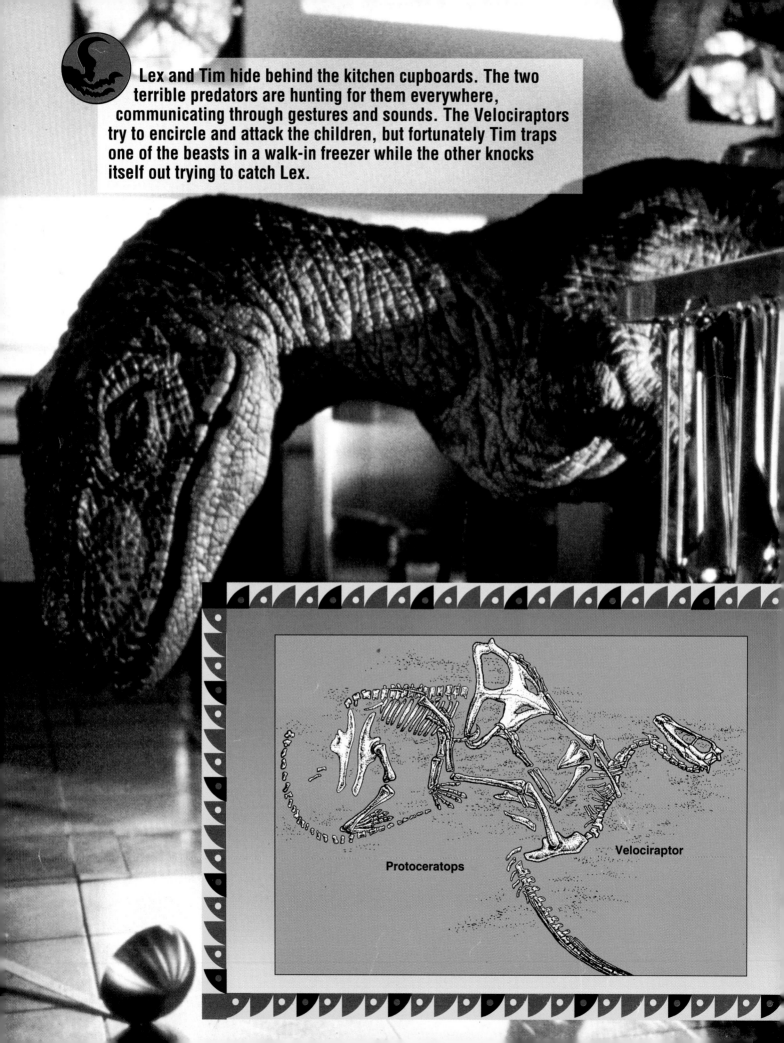

Lex and Tim hide behind the kitchen cupboards. The two terrible predators are hunting for them everywhere, communicating through gestures and sounds. The Velociraptors try to encircle and attack the children, but fortunately Tim traps one of the beasts in a walk-in freezer while the other knocks itself out trying to catch Lex.

Protoceratops

Velociraptor

Discoveries of new and complete meat-eating dinosaur skeletons are rare events. Velociraptor and many of the other members of the Dromaeosaur family have had fairly complete skeletons discovered over the last 80 years. Recently, an interesting fact was noticed about two of the Dromaeosaurs: Velociraptor and Deinonychus were discovered preserved with skeletons of their prey.

The illustration shows a Velociraptor skeleton (on the right) preserved with a skeleton of a Protoceratops (on the left). The fossil bones are locked in a very tight embrace. On closer examination, scientists discovered they had killed each other and were buried by a sandstorm soon after.

Although the Velociraptor was a tough predator, it seems it had to be careful when attacking a dinosaur of similar size. The plant-eating Protoceratops may have been protecting its nest of babies from the Velociraptor. When Dr. John Ostrom of Yale University in the United States discovered the skeletons of Deinonychus in the Cloverly badlands of Montana, he also uncovered the partial skeleton of a large plant-eating dinosaur known as Tenontosaurus. His interpretation of the discovery showed a group or pack of Deinonychus attacking the much larger Tenontosaurus. The fossils told the story of several Deinonychus being knocked down and crushed by the large and heavy plant-eater during the hunt. The Tenontosaurus was killed in the battle by the other Deinonychus. This is the first time that dinosaurs were discovered hunting in packs. Imagine a group of ferocious Velociraptors stalking in the forest, 75 million years ago . . .

Lex and Tim escape from the kitchen and make their way to the computer control room to find Dr. Grant and Dr. Sattler. Lex, a computer whiz, sits down at the controls and attempts to access the system and turn on the park's security locks. In the meantime, a Velociraptor has found their trail and is trying to get through the control room door.

Can Lex get the lock working before the animal pushes open the door? Dr. Grant and Dr. Sattler are desperately trying to hold it shut. Can they hold the door for long?

The senses of Velociraptor were very sharp. It was most likely a pack hunter that used some level of attack coordination requiring a form of communication with other pack members. Perhaps it used a combination of body movements and barking growls to communicate.

Its forward-looking eyes allowed it to track and pursue prey through the tangled forest. Velociraptor was probably very good at hearing the low-frequency sounds created by animals as they walked along.

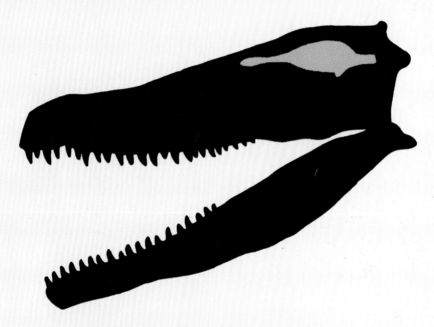

It is suspected that Velociraptor, like other members of the advanced meat-eating group, had an extremely powerful sense of smell. A large part of its brain was devoted to receiving and coordinating information from its sensitive nose. Smell can be the most effective way to track prey, even when the forest is thick or darkness falls the hunt can go on!

Dr. Grant and Dr. Sattler push with all their might to keep the Velociraptor from getting in. Just as Lex turns on the security locks, Dr. Grant, with a blow from his shoulder, slams the door shut. The Velociraptor growls in fury and charges the reinforced glass window, trying to burst through. Realizing the animal will soon break in, Dr. Grant removes a ceiling panel and gestures everyone to climb into the space above. They crawl, one behind the other, through the ventilation duct.

Suddenly, the Velociraptor's head bursts through the floor. Our heroes shake off the Velociraptor and escape, but not for long . . .

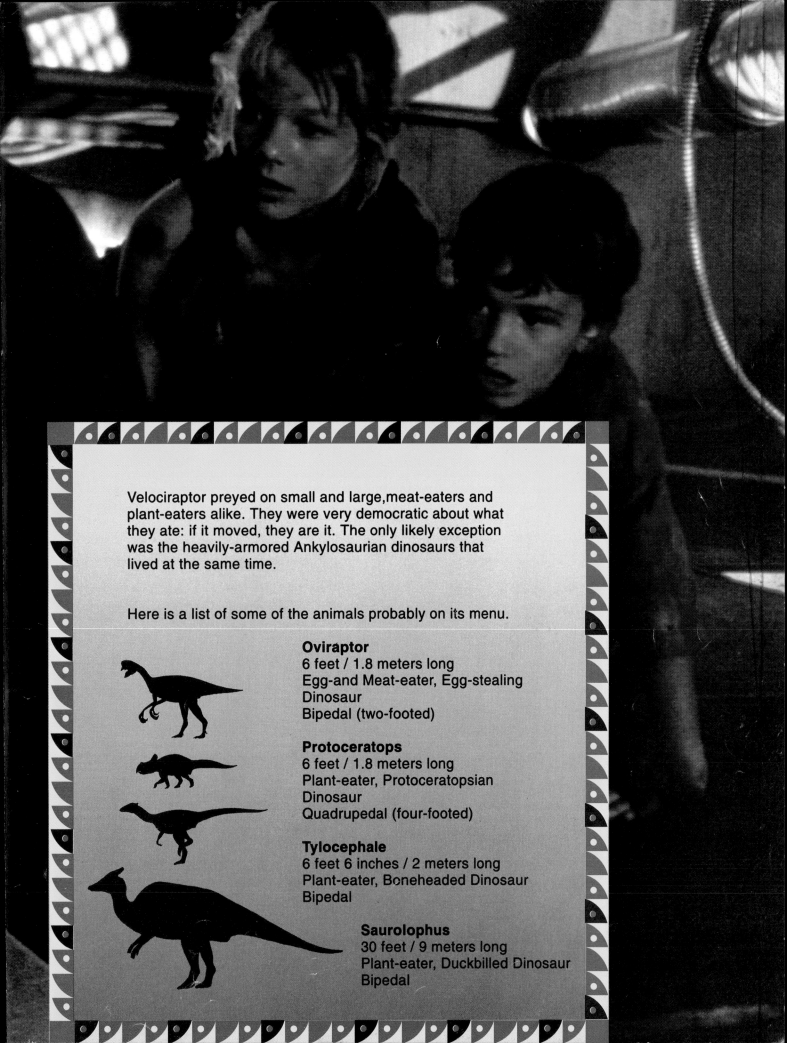

Velociraptor preyed on small and large,meat-eaters and plant-eaters alike. They were very democratic about what they ate: if it moved, they are it. The only likely exception was the heavily-armored Ankylosaurian dinosaurs that lived at the same time.

Here is a list of some of the animals probably on its menu.

Oviraptor
6 feet / 1.8 meters long
Egg-and Meat-eater, Egg-stealing Dinosaur
Bipedal (two-footed)

Protoceratops
6 feet / 1.8 meters long
Plant-eater, Protoceratopsian Dinosaur
Quadrupedal (four-footed)

Tylocephale
6 feet 6 inches / 2 meters long
Plant-eater, Boneheaded Dinosaur
Bipedal

Saurolophus
30 feet / 9 meters long
Plant-eater, Duckbilled Dinosaur
Bipedal

PREHISTORIC PENCIL HOLDER

You need :
Cardboard tube
Construction paper
Paint or markers

Draw the head, tail and feet of a dinosaur on construction paper. Color and cut them out.

Ask an adult for help to make a slit on each side of the tube, then color the tube.

Insert the head in one slit and the tail in the other. Then tape on the dinosaur feet to make your very own dinosaur pencil holder!

GLOSSARY

Bipedal	An animal that walks on its two back legs.
Dinosaur	An extinct group of land-dwelling animals closely related to birds and reptiles.
DNA	The short name for the genetic blueprints that determine the structure of a living organism.
Embryo	A fertilized animal egg.
Fossil	Any preserved evidence of ancient life.
Ornithopod	Any of the many types of small plant-eating dinosaurs.
Paleobotanist	A scientist who specifically studies fossil plants.
Paleontologist	A scientist who studies the evidence of ancient life.
Predator	Any organism that pursues or hunts animals for food.
Protoceratopsian	A family of small dinosaurs that gave rise to the Ceratopsians.
Quadrupedal	An animal that walks on all four legs.
Saurischian	One of the two main groups of dinosaurs; defined by the position of the bones in their hips. The bone positions resemble those of modern lizards, therefore they are called "lizard-hipped" or Saurischian.

Text
Lucie Duchesne and Andrew Leitch

Research
Andrew Leitch

Cover Illustration
Michel-Thomas Poulin

Illustrations
PaleoImage Ltd.

Art Direction
Studio de la Montagne
Louis C. Hébert

Desktop Publishing
Benoît Lafond and Line Godbout

Produced by
Group Potential Inc.

With photos from the movie
Jurassic Park

From a screenplay by
Michael Crichton et David Koepp

Based on a novel by
Michael Crichton

© Les Éditions Nublar Enr. All rights reserved. Printed in Canada.
TM & © 1993 Universal Studios, Inc. & Amblin Entertainment, Inc. All rights reserved.
JURASSIC PARK and JURASSIC PARK logo are registered trademarks of
Universal City Studios, Inc. & Amblin Entertainment, Inc.
Legal deposit Bibliothèque nationale du Québec, 1993.
Legal deposit Nationale Library of Canada, 1993. ISBN 2-921602-03-2